Dear Parents and Educators,

Welcome to Penguin Young Readers! As parents and educators, you know that each child develops at his or her own pace—in terms of speech, critical thinking, and, of course, reading. Penguin Young Readers recognizes this fact. As a result, each Penguin Young Readers book is assigned a traditional easy-to-read level (1–4) as well as a Guided Reading Level (A–P). Both of these systems will help you choose the right book for your child. Please refer to the back of each book for specific leveling information. Penguin Young Readers features esteemed authors and illustrators, stories about favorite characters, fascinating nonfiction, and more!

Scary Plants!

LEVEL 4

GUIDED READING LEVEL N

This book is perfect for a **Fluent Reader** who:
• can read the text quickly with minimal effort;
• has good comprehension skills;
• can self-correct (can recognize when something doesn't sound right); and
• can read aloud smoothly and with expression.

Here are some **activities** you can do during and after reading this book:
• Nonfiction: Nonfiction books deal with facts and events that are real. Talk about the elements of nonfiction. Discuss some of the facts you learned about these scary plants. Then, on a separate sheet of paper, write down facts about your favorite plants from this book.
• Comprehension: After reading the book, answer the following questions:
  • What does it mean if a plant is carnivorous? List a few ways plants catch insects.
  • Why do some plants have spines, prickles, or thorns?
  • What are the names of some poisonous flowers and fruit?

Remember, sharing the love of reading with a child is the best gift you can give!

—Sarah Fabiny, Editorial Director
　Penguin Young Readers program

*Penguin Young Readers are leveled by independent reviewers applying the standards developed by Irene Fountas and Gay Su Pinnell in *Matching Books to Readers: Using Leveled Books in Guided Reading*, Heinemann, 1999.

PENGUIN YOUNG READERS
An Imprint of Penguin Random House LLC

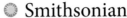 Smithsonian

This trademark is owned by the Smithsonian Institution and is registered in the U.S. Patent and
Trademark Office.

Smithsonian Enterprises:
Christopher Liedel, President
Carol LeBlanc, Senior Vice President, Education and Consumer Products
Brigid Ferraro, Vice President, Education and Consumer Products
Ellen Nanney, Licensing Manager
Kealy Gordon, Product Development Manager

Smithsonian Gardens:
Cynthia A. Brown, Supervisory Horticulturist Collections Specialist

Photo Credits: Cover and page 3: © bedo/Thinkstock; pages 4, 20, 21, 28–29 (top, center):
© Smithsonian Gardens; page 6: © Steve Hull Photography/Thinkstock; page 7 (top, left): © Christian
Fischer, (top, right): © IMNATURE/Thinkstock, (center): © Natarpat/Thinkstock, (bottom, left):
© arkira/Thinkstock, (bottom, right): © Sakaori; page 9: © Photodisc/Thinkstock; page 10: © Cathy
Keifer/Thinkstock; page 11 (top): © Rodney_X/Thinkstock, (bottom): © Jim1123/Thinkstock; page 13:
© NepGrower; page 14: © Argument/Thinkstock; page 15: © ArgenLant/Thinkstock; page 16:
© Jason Hollinger; page 17: © Flickr/Everglades NPS; pages 18–19: redstallion/Thinkstock; page 22:
© ToscaWhi/Thinkstock; page 23: © Lagui/Thinkstock; page 25: © Willem van Aken, CSIRO; page
26: © cturtletrax/Thinkstock; page 27: © PavlinaGab/Thinkstock; page 28 (bottom, left): © indigojt/
Thinkstock/, (bottom, right): © Thinkstock/Design Pics; page 29 (bottom): © Thinkstock/ChadHof7;
pages 30–31 (top): © Keith Kanoti, Maine Forest Service, Bugwood.org; page 31 (bottom): © mgdwn/
Thinkstock; page 32: © BasieB/Thinkstock; page 33: © FloWB/Thinkstock; page 34 (top and bottom):
© NajaShots/Thinkstock; page 35: © shakzu/Thinkstock; page 36 (left): © Purestock/Thinkstock,
(right): © Olga Rakhm/Thinkstock; page 37 (top, left): © Phil_Lowe/Thinkstock, (top, right):
© MIYAKO/amanaimagesRF/Thinkstock, (bottom, left): © Donald Eugene Hammond/Thinkstock,
(bottom, right): © Tikta Alik/Thinkstock; page 38: © JPhilipson/Thinkstock; page 39: © mazzzur/
Thinkstock; page 40: © lavoview/Thinkstock; page 41 (top): © pornsakampa/Thinkstock, (bottom):
© Noppasin Wongchum/Thinkstock; page 43 (top): © Nickel_Bell/Thinkstock, (bottom):
© paolomarchetti/Thinkstock; page 44 (top): © bkkm/Thinkstock, (bottom): © Ryan Capson/
Thinkstock; page 45: © shihina/Thinkstock; page 46: © Marilyn Barbone/Thinkstock; page 47:
© Nick White/Thinkstock; page 48: © richcarey/Thinkstock.

Library of Congress Cataloging-in-Publication Data is available

ISBN 9780451533715 (pbk)   10 9 8 7 6 5 4 3 2 1
ISBN 9780451533722 (hc)   10 9 8 7 6 5 4 3 2 1

Smithsonian
SCARY PLANTS!

by Janet Lawler

Penguin Young Readers
An Imprint of Penguin Random House

Contents

Here a Plant,
There a Plant . . .

Plants grow all over the world.
There are hundreds of thousands
of kinds.

Some are as tiny as a grain of sand.
Others are as tall as buildings. They can
live in sidewalk cracks, on mountains, in
lakes and oceans, and even under snow.

Plants are one of the five main groups of living things. Vegetables, flowers, and trees are all plants.

We could not live without plants. They help make the **oxygen** we breathe. They are used for food, clothing, and **shelter**.

Many plants smell nice, look pretty, or taste good. But not all plants. Some of them can seem scary!

Trapped

Insects should steer clear of **carnivorous plants**! (say: car-NIV-or-us) These plants capture and eat bugs.

The leaves of a Venus flytrap open wide. There are short hairs on the leaves. When an insect crawls in, it touches the hairs.

Snap!

A Venus flytrap leaf closes in less than a second. The insect is stuck inside. The plant **digests** it.

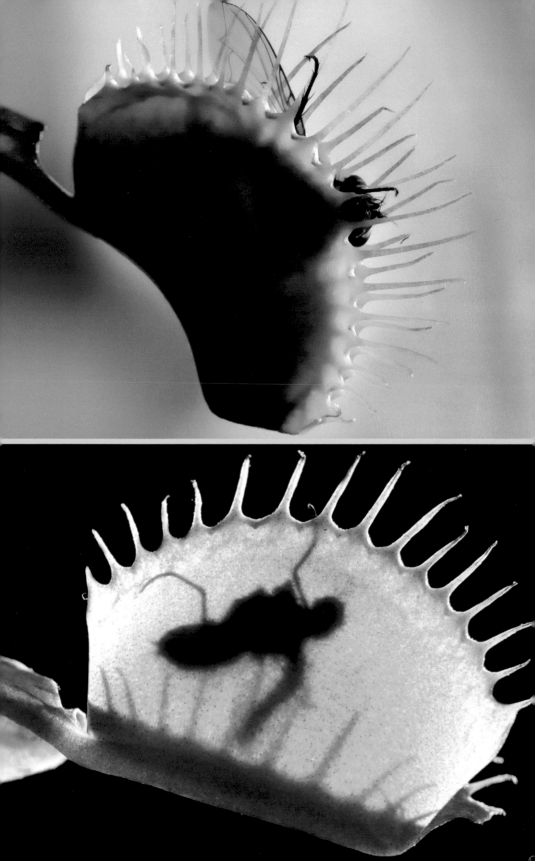

Pitcher plants make **nectar**. It smells sweet. Insects like the smell and come for a sip.

But a sip becomes a slip!

Insects slide down into the pitcher plant's slippery cup. They fall into a pool at the bottom. They drown and become food for the plant.

Tiny hairs on sundew leaves are covered with a very sticky sap. An insect that comes too close gets stuck.

The tiny hairs curl over the bug. Now it's really trapped! Juices in the sundew turn its **prey** into a meal.

Bladderworts work like underwater vacuum cleaners. These floating plants have no roots. But they do have small pod-like traps.

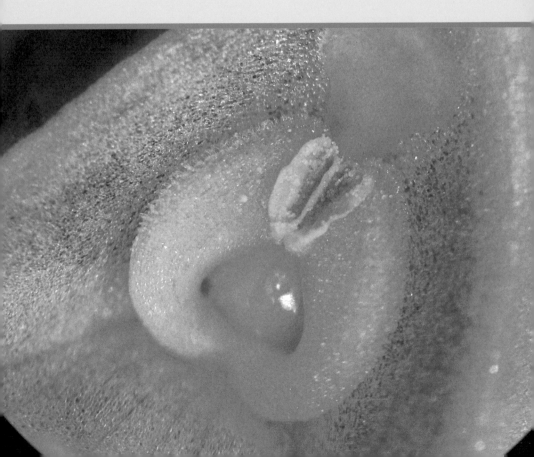

When prey triggers a pod's trap door,
the bladderwort sucks it right in.

Ouch!

Spines, prickles, and thorns make a plant look scary. They help protect plants from being eaten.

Blackberry stems have sharp prickles. These thorn-like points can poke, prick, and tear skin.

Blackberry stems can grow as long as 35 feet. They often bend as they grow. When they touch the ground, new roots take hold. Soon there is a thick **tangle**. Most animals and people can't get through.

Cactus plants come in many shapes and sizes. Most have sharp, needle-like spines.

The spines are really the leaves of a cactus. They help the plant **survive**.

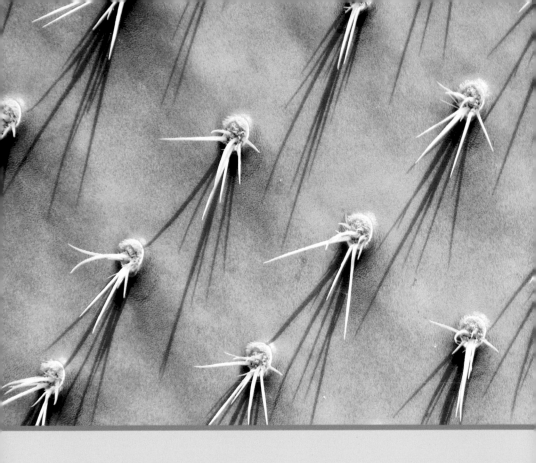

Are those small, fuzzy dots?

No! Don't brush against them!

The prickly pear cactus is covered with many small spines. These tiny spines are barbed and hook into fur or skin.

The Australian Gympie-Gympie tree has pretty, heart-shaped leaves.

Beware! They are pretty deadly!

The leaves, stems, and fruit of this plant are covered with stinging hairs. These hairs can prick animals and people. They squirt poison into whatever touches them. That is very, very painful.

Stinging nettles are also covered with needle-like hairs. Brush against this plant and stinging sap goes into your skin. You'll feel like you were stung by a wasp or a bee.

Don't Touch!

Some plants look like trouble. Others look harmless, but they are not!

Poison ivy contains oil that causes an itchy skin rash and blisters. This oil sticks to skin, clothes, and even fur. Touching a pet that brushed against this plant can give you the rash!

Poison ivy often grows in clumps. Its vines spread along the ground or climb walls, fences, buildings, trees, and other plants.

Poison ivy leaves have three pointed parts.

Poison oak and poison sumac have
the same oil that is in poison ivy. Air can
carry drops of this oil. If any of these
plants burn, the oil will be in the smoke.
It is dangerous to breathe it in.

Poison sumac

Poison oak bush

The giant hogweed is a big plant—and a big problem!

It has large white flowers.

It can grow up to 14 feet high.

It likes **moist** soil but grows in many places.

Stay away!

A gooey sap oozes from the giant hogweed's stem and leaves. It can drip onto a person's skin. When the sun's rays hit the sap, it will cause painful blisters and burns.

Every part of the manchineel tree
is poisonous. Its leaves, bark, and sap
cause severe blisters. Its fruit looks

like little green apples. But they are dangerous and deadly to eat.

Manchineel sap was once used on poison darts and arrows.

No Eating

Plants may grow flowers or fruit that look good to eat. Holly, bittersweet, and yew have colorful berries.

But they are poisonous!

So are many pretty flowers such as buttercups, daffodils, and morning glories.

Holly

Buttercups

Bittersweet

Daffodils

Don't eat any plants
unless an adult says it's okay.

Morning glories

Yew

Stinky

Not all plants smell nice. Some smell so bad that they are called **corpse** flowers. The flowers smell like a dead cow on a hot day. Or rotting fish. Or dog poop.

The awful **odor** attracts flies and other insects that carry **pollen** to and from other flowers.

One kind of corpse plant has the world's biggest flower. This flower can be three feet wide and weigh twenty pounds.

World's biggest flower

Plants can also make stinky fruit.

The durian looks like a large, spiky ball. The soft inside of this Asian fruit smells rotten.

Some places have laws against bringing durians into hotels, buses, trains, or taxis.

What Is *That*?

Sometimes plants only *look* weird or scary.

The tree tumbo grows in some African deserts. It has only two leaves! Over time, these leaves bend, twist, tear, and shred. They form a jumbled pile.

A tree tumbo may live more than 1,000 years.

A tree tumbo looks like a leathery octopus lying on the desert sand.

White baneberry

Black bat flower

44

The white baneberry plant's berries look like eyeballs growing on a deep-pink stem. The plant is nicknamed Doll Eyes.

The black bat flower of Asia looks like a bat with its wings outspread.

Living stone plants look like small rocks. They blend in with the ground. Animals searching for food often pass them by.

Living stones store water in their fat leaves.

Everywhere a Plant

Plants sprout in woods, water, or wherever they can. They bloom in backyards, parks, and gardens.

Keep a lookout for scary and not-so-scary plants everywhere you go.

Plants: They'll grow on you!

Glossary

carnivorous plants: insect-eating plants

corpse: a dead body

digests: breaks down something so it becomes food

moist: slightly wet

nectar: a sweet liquid made by plants

odor: a smell

oxygen: gas that is a part of air; it has no color, taste, or smell

pollen: a dust-like part of a plant that helps it make seeds

prey: a living thing that another living thing uses for food

shelter: a place to live or hide

survive: to continue to live

tangle: twisted together in a messy way

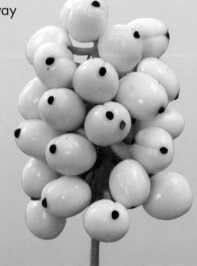